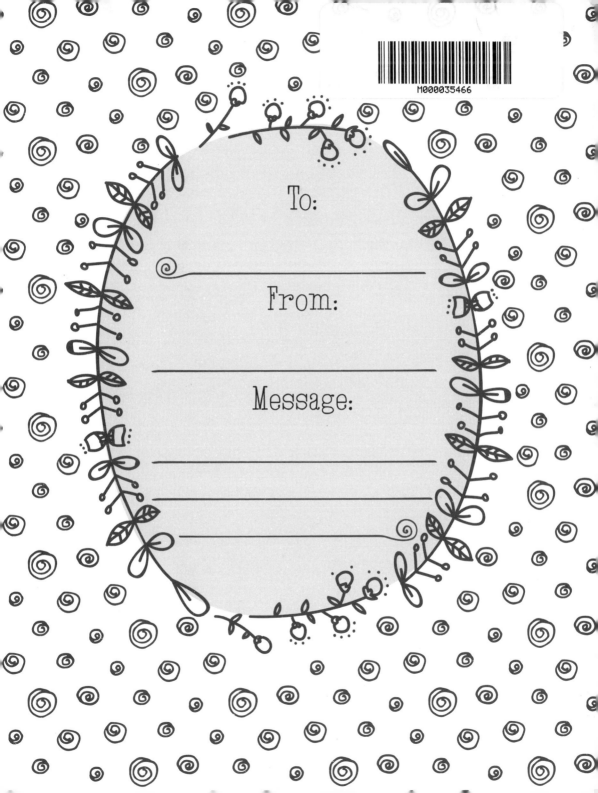

To:

_____

From:

_____

Message:

_____

_____

_____

Doodle Devotions for Girls

Published by Christian Art Publishers
PO Box 1599, Vereeniging, 1930, RSA

© 2019
First edition 2019

Designed by Christian Art Publishers

Images used under license from Shutterstock.com

Scripture quotations are taken from the *Holy Bible*, New Living Translation,
copyright © 1996, 2004, 2007, 2013, 2015 by Tyndale House Foundation.
Used by permission of Tyndale House Publishers, Carol Stream, Illinois 60188.
All rights reserved.

Printed in China

ISBN 978-1-4321-2711-4

21 22 23 24 25 26 27 28 29 30 – 19 18 17 16 15 14 13 12 11 10

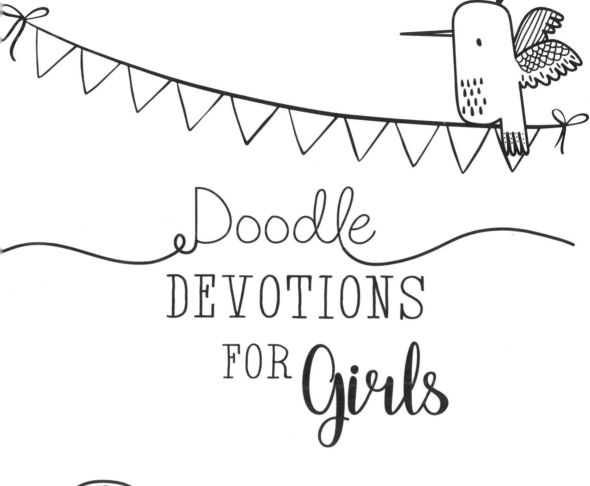

Doodle
DEVOTIONS
FOR *Girls*

NANCY TAYLOR

CHRISTIAN ART PUBLISHERS

CONTENTS

Week 5 – Family Matters

Week 6 – Friends and Foes

Week 7 – True Love

Week 8 – True Beauty

INTRODUCTION

Right off the bat, I need to confess something to you. I'm pretty old. I even have some grey hair. But don't stop reading—I really am qualified to write this book. You see, I live with three teenage girls, an almost-teen boy, and a little girl who will be a teen before I know it. They all read this book and said it works. Plus, I remember more about my own teenage years than you might think.

I don't know about you, but one of my favorite things to do is doodle. You know, little words and pictures written in fun colors and fancy letters. My girls love it too. One day I thought, *I wonder if we can find a way to use doodling to draw closer to God?* And so this book was born. Here you'll find devotionals on 12 themes, each with 5 related entries. You can do it over 12 weeks, with one entry for each weekday, or you can do it at your own pace.

I hope that as you read and doodle in this book you will learn a little about yourself—who you are and who you want to be. But even more than that, I hope you will learn about God—who He is and what He wants you to be. The great thing is, the more you discover about God, the more you will understand about yourself and the more content you will be with who you are.

Now, let's get doodling!

Week

1

God and Me ...

A BIG, BIG GOD

If you have ever gazed over the edge of the Grand Canyon in Arizona, or climbed to the top of a mountain and admired the view, you have grasped a little bit of how BIG God is. He made everything that exists, out of nothing, with just a breath. Think about that for a minute. First there was nothing but God, and then He called into being everything that we see and hear and touch and taste.

Now, it stands to reason that if God made everything, then He also has the right to tell us how things work and what to do. It's kind of like if you paint a picture or write a story; you get to call the shots in that world you've created. God gets to call the shots in our world, too. That means first of all that He has power to do anything He wants, and second of all we should obey Him and make Him King over our lives.

That might sound a little scary at first—give God control over my life? Do what He says in the Bible even if I don't want to? But in addition to being BIG, God is also GOOD. Perfectly, completely, totally good. And that means that we can trust Him to do good things for us and trust that His ways are best.

The LORD is God, and he created the heavens
and earth and put everything in place . . . "I am the LORD,"
he says, "and there is no other."

Isaiah 45:18

Your head is probably spinning right now. These are big,
confusing thoughts about a BIG God. Before we go any farther,
use this space to write down some questions you have about God,
the world, yourself, or whatever is keeping you up at night. At the
end of the book, you can come back to this page and see if any of
your questions have been answered.

THE BIG PROBLEM

Let's pick up where we left off. . . . God created everything (out of nothing!), and for that reason He has the right to make the rules for how we should live. The problem is, we don't follow His rules. The very first humans, Adam and Eve, had only one rule to obey. God gave them a whole garden paradise to live in, with all their needs met, and told them that all they had to do was not eat the fruit from one tree. It seems like it would be easy to keep one rule, but Satan came in and tempted them, and suddenly they thought that fruit was just too good to pass up. They doubted that God had their best interests at heart, they believed their way was better, and so they traded the perfect world God had given them for a piece of fruit.

Suddenly everything changed. First off, they couldn't live in the garden anymore or talk with God face-to-face. Because God is perfect, He can't be with sinners. So there was separation between people and God. In addition, they would die. The Bible says, "the wages of sin is death" (Romans 6:23). In the meantime, life on earth would be full of pain, shame, and sin. All of our problems in life boil down to the fact that there is sin in the world. Your sin, my sin, and the effects of sin on the earth bring us suffering, shame, and separation from God.

Fortunately, God had a rescue plan, and we'll get to that tomorrow. But today let's think about sin. Think of something you're tempted by, even though you know it's wrong, and write down the lies Satan is whispering in your ear that make it seem desirable. Sometimes seeing a lie written down helps us not be tempted by it anymore.

If we claim we have no sin, we are only fooling ourselves and not living in the truth. But if we confess our sins to him, he is faithful and just to forgive us our sins and to cleanse us from all wickedness. 1 John 1:8-9

JESUS MADE
A WAY

The big problem of sin is no match for our BIG God. He had a plan all along to pay the penalty for our sin Himself. You see, we deserve death and an eternity in hell because we fall short of God's perfect standard, but He sent the perfect sacrifice—His own Son—to pay our debt for us. Jesus, though He was God, came to earth as a baby, grew up just like we do, and then was crucified on a wooden cross, died, and was buried.

But there was one key difference between Jesus' life and ours: He was perfect. He was tempted, just like we are, but He never gave in. He lived the perfect life that we are unable to live. And because He completely obeyed God the Father in all things, He was able to pay the penalty for sin once and for all. His death means that we can be declared innocent! It's like when a judge passes down a sentence for a fine to be paid, but then pays the fine herself on behalf of the criminal.

Romans 5:18 explains how this works: "Adam's one sin brings condemnation for everyone, but Christ's one act of righteousness brings a right relationship with God and new life for everyone." In other words, the sin of Adam made us all sinners, but the death of Jesus took away all the guilt of the whole world.

Using the space below, write or draw what Jesus' death on the cross means to you. Have you taken hold of the salvation He offers you to be free of guilt and live with Him forever?

Jesus was handed over to die because of our sins, and he was raised to life to make us right with God.

Romans 4:25

Have you ever tried to go a whole day without sinning? It's not just hard—it's impossible! I don't know about you, but I can't even go a whole hour without some sinful thought or careless word or just plain meanness spoiling it. We all sin. But that's where God's grace comes in. Grace means "unmerited favor." God knows how sinful we are because He knows everything about us, but He gives us grace instead of the punishment we deserve.

This is the good news that the whole Bible is about: We can be saved from our sin and saved from the penalty our sins deserve (death and hell) because our salvation depends not on us, but on God. We can't earn our way to heaven, but God graciously makes a way for us to be saved. Paul wrote in his letter to the Ephesians, "God saved you by his grace when you believed. And you can't take credit for this; it is a gift from God. Salvation is not a reward for the good things we have done, so none of us can boast about it" (2:8-9).

No matter how badly you mess up, God's grace is for you. He wants to forgive you and to save you from your sin. All you have to do is believe that Jesus is God and trust in His death on the cross to save you.

God saved you by his *Grace* when you believed & you can't take credit for this; it is a *GIFT from God.*

EPHESIANS 2:8

God's free gift of salvation is yours for the taking.
Have you trusted Him with your heart and your life?
On the gift box above, write out a prayer of thanks
for the grace you have in Jesus.

A NEW CREATION

My favorite season is spring, because I love seeing the yellow buds on the forsythia bushes and the teeny-tiny leaves on the trees. And who can resist the baby animals that emerge as the weather warms up? There's just something about new life that brings joy to our hearts and a fresh optimism to our outlook.

When you became a Christian by believing in Jesus, you received new life. Everything about you was affected by that decision. Paul wrote, "Anyone who belongs to Christ has become a new person. The old life is gone; a new life has begun!" (2 Corinthians 5:17). Your priorities changed—now instead of wanting your own way, you choose God's way. Your attitude changed—now instead of seeing the bad things in the world and despairing, you have hope that one day God will make everything right again. Your affections changed, too—now you love God and His people.

Deciding to follow Jesus made you a new person. Now your job is to live like the person He made you to be. Choose actions that reflect God's character to the people around you. Foster hope and joy in your heart rather than gloom. Every moment, your choices reflect either your new life in Christ or your old life focused on sin and self. Be a springtime Christian!

Anyone who belongs to Christ has become a new person. The old life is gone; a new life has begun!

2 Corinthians 5:17

Would the people you are closest to say that you are a springtime creation, full of life and hope and joy because of what God has done for you? Doodle some happy images that remind you of new life, and ask God to help you live as the new creation you are in Him.

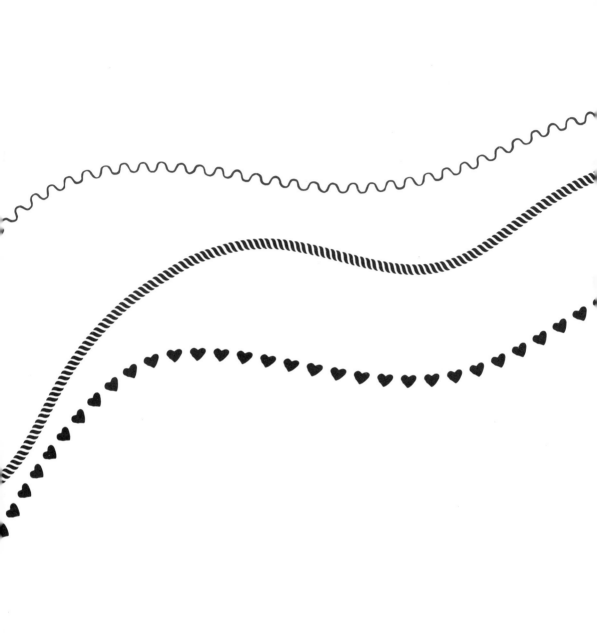

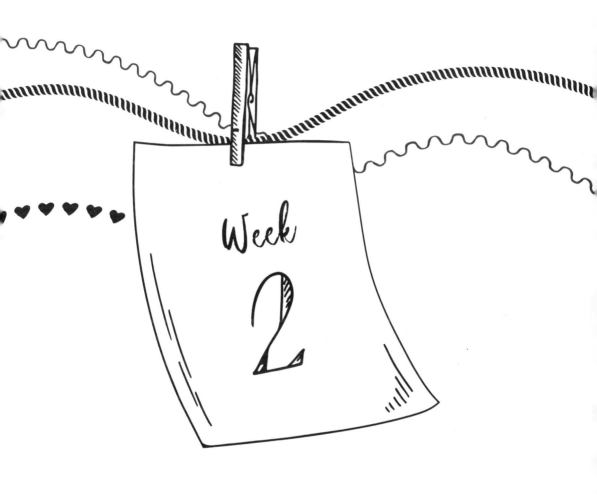

Week

2

Who Am I?

A VERY SIGNIFICANT SPECK

Do you ever look up at the sky and feel very small? I do, especially at night. There are so many stars and planets, so far away, and I am just a little speck on this great big globe. How is it possible that the God who made all of this cares for little old me? But He does!

King David felt this way too. He wrote, "When I look at the night sky and see the work of your fingers—the moon and the stars you set in place—what are mere mortals that you should think about them, human beings that you should care for them? Yet you made them only a little lower than God and crowned them with glory and honor" (Psalm 8:3-5).

It's true—the God of the universe cares for YOU! He stamped you with His own image, declaring that you belong to Him, and because you are made in God's image, you share a little bit of His glory. Far from being an insignificant speck in the universe, you are lovingly and carefully made by the Creator of all things, and your very existence brings Him joy. The Bible even says that He sings songs of joy over you (Zephaniah 3:17). So next time you think you're unimportant, remember that the all-powerful Creator who made everything says that you are important to Him.

Color in these stars and add some of your own.
As you create your universe, think of God masterfully
creating all the stars and planets . . . and you!

For the LORD your God . . .
will take delight in you with *gladness.*
With his love,
he will calm all your fears.
He will *rejoice*
over you with joyful songs.

Zephaniah 3:17

Mirror, Mirror, on the Wall

When you look in the mirror, what kinds of things do you say to yourself? Are you always tearing yourself down, pointing out your flaws and wishing for a smaller nose or more defined cheekbones? Do you wish you had the same talents and abilities as someone else, and belittle your own capabilities? We've all done that at some point.

But do you know what God sees when He looks at you? He sees a precious, beautiful daughter. He made you exactly as He intended, with a particular color of eyes and the perfect chin shape and all the right abilities to do everything He wants you to do. And He doesn't make mistakes. The Bible says, "You made all the delicate, inner parts of my body and knit me together in my mother's womb. Thank you for making me so wonderfully complex! Your workmanship is marvelous—how well I know it" (Psalm 139:13-14).

Next time you look in the mirror, thank God for the way He knit you together. You are His beautiful, beloved daughter, made exactly the way He wanted. He declares His creation "very good," and you should do the same!

You made all the delicate, inner parts of my body and knit me together in my mother's womb. Thank *you* for making me so WONDERFULLY COMPLEX! Your workmanship is *Marvelous* —how well I know it.

Psalm 139:13-14

On this mirror, write down words that describe all the wonderful things that make you who you are. What do you love? What is unique about you? Thank God for His amazing workmanship!

WHY AM I HERE?

Have you ever wondered—to yourself or even out loud to a friend—why you're here? Here you are, hurtling through a vast solar system, on this huge earth, among 7.4 billion people. Why did God make you in the first place, and why did He place you in your town, in your neighborhood, in your family? These questions kind of make my head spin.

You were created with a purpose. First there is a big purpose to your life, the same purpose each person on earth has: you were created to praise and glorify God, because He delights in you. Colossians 1:16 says, "Everything was created through him [Jesus] and for him." This echoes the Psalmist's words: The LORD delights in his people" (Psalm 149:4). Your very existence brings God pleasure, and that is purpose enough to keep on getting up each morning, even when it feels like each day looks a whole lot like the previous one.

But there is more. You are created to respond to God's love with worship, a whole life lived in love and praise to God. Paul wrote, "Whatever you do, do it all for the glory of God" (1 Corinthians 10:31). Each day, you have the opportunity to fulfill God's purpose for you as you choose to obey and honor Him. Ephesians 2:10 summarizes both aspects of our purpose with these words: "We are God's masterpiece. He has created us anew in Christ Jesus, so we can do the good things he planned for us long ago."

Color in this page, and then on the inside space write or draw some of the things God has called you to do. How can you fulfill your purpose today?

We are God's masterpiece. He has created us anew in Christ Jesus, so we can do the good things he planned for us long ago.

Ephesians 2:10

WHY DO I KEEP MESSING UP?

Christians in the last century used to talk about "besetting sins." It's kind of an old-fashioned term, but it's a very modern-day problem. It basically means the sins that keep on tripping you up. For me, it's impatience. No matter how hard I try, I just can't seem to slow down and wait for God to work things out or for people to do what I think they should do. I want things to be done now, not later.

Each of us has areas where we are more tempted than others. Satan knows just which buttons to push, and his goal is to get us so discouraged in our battle against sin that we just give up and rationalize it away. "It's not that big of a deal," we say. "No matter how hard I try, I can't seem to get it right, so I might as well stop trying. God will forgive me."

God doesn't want us to give up like that! He has given us the Holy Spirit to live inside us and empower us to do what is right. The Spirit pricks our conscience to remind us of what is right, and God promises that for any temptation we face, there is a way out. Even our besetting sins. Take hold of God's promises today, and keep fighting against the sins that so easily trip you up.

The temptations in your life are no different from what others experience. And God is faithful. He will not allow the temptation to be more than you can stand. When you are tempted, he will show you a way out so that you can endure.

1 Corinthians 10:13

In the space above, jot down some ways you can avoid the sins that seem to keep tripping you up. Maybe there is a new habit you could put in place, or some situations you can avoid.

THE GIFT OF YOU

We often talk about the gift of salvation—the offer God makes to exchange our sinfulness for His righteousness so we can be free from the grip of sin. But did you know that you are also a gift yourself? Each Christian has one or more spiritual gifts. These are special abilities that the Holy Spirit places inside you when you put your faith in Jesus. You have always had talents or things you're good at. But when you decided to trust in Jesus you acquired new gifts, supernatural abilities that help you to serve God and His people.

The most important thing to know about spiritual gifts is that every Christian has them, and they are given for you to help other believers. Examples of spiritual gifts are: wisdom (special discernment about how to apply God's Word to real-life situations), teaching (the ability to communicate spiritual truth in such a way that people understand it in a new way), helping (noticing when people need help and jumping in to serve), encouragement (finding ways to bring joy to others), and faith (unusual trust in God).

There are many others listed in Scripture, and probably the lists in Scripture don't even include all the gifts the Spirit gives. Have you ever thought about what your spiritual gifts are? Be on the lookout for times when people say that something you do or say has really encouraged or helped them—that might be a clue.

A spiritual gift is given to each of us so we can help each other.

1 Corinthians 12:7

You may sometimes feel like you don't have a lot to offer, especially while you're young, but you have gifts that your church needs! After you color in the gift bag, jot some spiritual "presents" you can give to other believers this week.

Week
3

Oh, the Joy!

ABUNDANT LIFE

Some people have an image of Christians being all doom and gloom and legalistic rule-keepers. They think of God as a judge who is poised to come down with His gavel and punish us for what we've done wrong. To them, religion is about a bunch of boring, outdated rules.

But that's not Christianity! Actually, Christianity isn't a religion at all. It's a relationship with God, made possible because Jesus' death on the cross enables us to be declared "not guilty!" even though we have sinned. Jesus said, "My purpose is to give them a rich and satisfying life" (John 10:10). Christians should be the happiest people on earth, because they have found the way to true life and freedom from sin.

God offers you abundant life—overflowing with good gifts. Now, that doesn't mean you have lots of "stuff." What it does mean is that you have all you could ever want of what truly matters, the things that will make you truly happy. Things like peace that passes understanding, joy even in the midst of suffering, forgiveness for all your sin, and eternal life in heaven to look forward to. When you think of all that God has given you, you can't help but have a smile on your face and a spring in your step.

"The thief's purpose is to steal and kill and destroy. My *purpose* is to give (BELIEVERS) a rich and satisfying life."

John 10:10

In the space above, doodle some images of what abundant life means to you.

THE PEACE OF OBEDIENCE

In the last devotional we talked about the rich and satisfying life Jesus offers us. But there is a catch: we will only have that abundant life if we are walking in step with Him. If we're trying to go our own way, choosing to do things we know are wrong, we will experience heartache and bad consequences for our actions. God knows how life works best, so if we are obeying Him then we'll have the best life possible.

That doesn't mean that the path of obedience is always the easiest path. In fact, often it is the most difficult. Your reputation may take a hit if you are kind to the most unpopular girl in your school, but inside you'll feel peace because you will know you're doing the right thing. You may get in trouble if you confess that you lied about where you were and who you were with, but you will be building a better relationship with your parents and eventually that will pay off in more freedom for you. You may lose your spot on the team if you tell your coach that your teammates are cheating, but your conscience will be clean. And who knows? Maybe God will help you find an even better team.

Are you looking for more peace in your life? Line your behavior up with God's Word, obeying Him even when it is hard, and you will have peace in your heart.

"Oh, that you had listened to
MY COMMANDS!
Then you would have had *peace*
flowing like a gentle river
& RIGHTEOUSNESS
rolling over you like waves in the sea."

Isaiah 48:18

Draw some footprints on the path above,
and inside each one write a command from the
Bible that you are trying to obey.

TRUTH VERSUS FEELING

I have a terrible sense of direction. It's so bad that if I am trying to navigate in unfamiliar territory I often deliberately go in the opposite of whatever direction I think I should—and usually the opposite of what my intuition says turns out to be the right way. There's nothing wrong with having a bad sense of direction . . . as long as you're willing to ask for help when you need it.

Sometimes we have a bad sense of direction about life, too. It's tempting to make choices based on our emotions, but often our feelings lead us into sin. Emotions are fickle and shallow, and they rarely line up with objective truth. A better way to live is to navigate our lives according to God's Word. Psalm 119:105 says, "Your word is a lamp to guide my feet and a light for my path." Another Scripture verse tells us that God's Word will endure forever (Isaiah 40:8).

The Bible is the only enduring, objective truth we can find. One day everything else will fade away, but God's Word will still be standing and will still be pointing the way to truth. So next time you have a choice to make, point yourself back to the Bible and do what it says—even if your feelings are telling you something else. That's a rock-solid foundation to build your life on!

"Anyone who listens to my teaching and
follows it is wise,
like a person who builds a
house on solid rock."

Matthew 7:24

In the space on the Bible,
write your favorite Scripture verse
in fancy letters. Think about how
that verse helps you live God's way.

THE ONE WHO CALMS THE STORM

Jesus and His disciples had spent the day with thronging crowds, thousands of people anxious to hear Jesus' teaching. Jesus suggested they take some time off and head to the other side of the lake, and no doubt the disciples were eager for some peace and quiet and time alone with their Master.

Then came the unexpected: a huge storm that threatened to overturn their boat and kill them all. And even more unexpected, somehow Jesus was sleeping through it all! They couldn't believe it: "Teacher, don't you care that we are going to drown?"

The disciples' words sound an awful lot like some of my prayers. "Lord, don't You care about this big problem that is keeping me up at night?" Jesus silenced both the disciples and the storm with just a few words: "Peace! Be still!" and instantly everything was calm. The calm— and Jesus' great power—was even more terrifying to the disciples than the storm had been.

I don't know what storms you're facing right now. Perhaps your family is in trouble or you've made a big mess of your life or you have a friend who is terribly sick. Whatever your storm, whatever is keeping you up at night, tell Jesus about it. Ask Him to calm your heart even in the midst of the storm, and to demonstrate His power over every difficulty you face.

Don't worry about anything; instead, pray about everything. Tell God what you need, and thank him for all he has done. Then you will experience God's peace, which exceeds anything we can understand. His peace will guard your hearts and minds as you live in Christ Jesus.

PHILIPPIANS 4:6-7

You can read the story about Jesus calming the storm in Mark 4:35-41. As you reflect on this story, doodle about the things you are worried about. Ask Jesus to bring peace to your heart and calming power to your life.

WHEN LIFE HURTS

Maybe the last devotional brought to mind some concerns and problems that are heavy on your heart. Sometimes our problems are so big that we just can't deal with them on our own. Perhaps you have had terrible things done to you, and you wonder if it is your fault. Maybe you are so worried about something that it is affecting your sleep or eating habits. Maybe things look really dark and you can't see how they could get better. Girls sometimes have so much pain in their hearts that they start harming themselves in some way, or they think about harming themselves.

If that is your story, know that it is not your fault and you are not alone. The evil that is in the world because of sin affects each one of us, and sometimes it creates such deep pain that it is more than we can bear alone.

If that sounds like you, please get help, now. Tell your story to someone you can trust—your parents, an older sibling, a pastor or youth leader, a counselor, a trusted teacher or coach—all of these people want to help you. But they can't help you if you don't speak out. Take that first brave step and talk about what's going on in your heart.

Use this coloring page to calm your mind and heart after a hard day.

Give your burdens to the LORD, and he will take care of you.
He will not permit the godly to slip and fall.

Psalm 55:22

Week 4

Contentment

AN ATTITUDE OF GRATITUDE

Do your parents ever make you send someone a thank-you note? Even if you secretly despise the ugly green sweater Aunt Gertrude knitted for you and never intend to wear it, it is good manners to take a few minutes to thank her for her kindness—in writing. After all, it's the thought that counts, right?

Even if you have a good habit of writing thank-you notes, I bet you often go through a day with little thought for the gifts God has given you, and even less intention to actually thank Him. That beautiful sunrise you saw on the way to school? That was a gift from God. The kind word from a friend? That was God too. In fact, the Bible tells us that EVERY good and perfect gift is from God (James 1:17).

Scientists tell us that when we express appreciation we actually change our brain chemistry. Going through the motions of gratitude changes our outlook. So not only are you praising God when you thank Him for His good gifts, you are also helping your attitude. And more likely than not, when you are grateful the people around you will find themselves feeling more grateful too.

I will praise you, LORD, with all my heart; I will tell of all the marvelous things you have done.

Psalm 9:1

Using the space above, write a thank-you note to God, thanking Him for all His good gifts to you. Maybe you want to find a blank notebook and start a gratitude journal, where you record three things you're thankful for each day.

DO YOU TRUST YOUR DAD?

Think about the last thing you asked your parents for. Was it a ride to a friend's house? A cookie? An awesome toy that you thought was too expensive? Parents like to give things to their kids. In fact, that's why they say no to some things—they want what's best for you, and sometimes they know that something you want isn't actually good for you.

When He was teaching about prayer, Jesus reminded people that parents give their children good things, and then He said, "If you sinful people know how to give good gifts to your children, how much more will your heavenly Father give good gifts to those who ask him" (Matthew 7:11). You see, God is the perfect Father. And He knows everything—including what is best for you. Sometimes He doesn't give you what you want, no matter how much you plead with Him. But He does always give you what you need.

So the big question in life is, will you trust your heavenly Father? Do you believe that He can do anything, that He loves you, and that He is perfect? If you believe all that, then you can trust Him even when you don't get the answer you want. Even when you don't make the team, or people hurt you, or you get sick, or a loved one dies. Even then, God is your good Father, and He is loving you and working things out for your good.

We know that **God** CAUSES EVERYTHING to work together for the GOOD of those who *love* **GOD** & are called according to HIS PURPOSE FOR THEM.

Romans 8:28

In the space above, write or doodle some of the things you're trusting God for even though you don't understand why He's allowing what He is. Pray that He will help you trust Him even when life hurts.

WHERE IS YOUR HOME?

Think about where you live. What's the best thing about it? What's the worst thing about it? I have lived my whole life within a few miles of the house where I was born, and I love that I feel so at home here. Even so, Wheaton, Illinois, isn't my real home.

Regardless of whether we've spent our whole lives on the move or have lived at the same address since we were born, our home is temporary. It's not going to last forever. The good news is that God is building a home for us in heaven, and that's where we really belong. Jesus told His disciples, "I am going to prepare a place for you. When everything is ready, I will come and get you, so that you will always be with me where I am" (John 14:2-3).

Our heavenly home will be better than anything we can imagine. There will be no more sickness or sorrow or sin or tears. We will be in the presence of God Himself, and we will have glorious new bodies that are perfected in Him. We will be fully satisfied and happy in our inmost being because we will finally be who we were made to be and enjoying fellowship with the One who made us and redeemed us. That is something to look forward to, even if our earthly homes are nearly perfect.

We are citizens of heaven,
where the Lord Jesus Christ lives.
And we are eagerly waiting for
him to return as our Savior.

Philippians 3:20

What are you thankful for about where you live now? What are
you most looking forward to about heaven? In the space above, write
words or doodles that help you be content where you are now while
also looking forward to your true forever home in heaven.

COMPARE AND DESPAIR

Whenever I start to complain about something someone else has that I wish I had (a special talent, a new technological marvel, or a fun new relationship), my friend always says, "Compare and despair." What she means is that no matter how great a life we have, if we start to compare what we have to what someone else has, we will always find something to despair about. There is always greener grass somewhere, and we often don't have to look farther than the fence around our yard.

On the other hand, if we focus on all the good things in our lives, we will find plenty to be thankful for. As we've already seen, God is our loving and perfect heavenly Father who gives us exactly what is best for us. Psalm 84:11 says, "The LORD will withhold no good thing from those who do what is right." In other words, if it is in our best interest to have something, God will give it to us. And if we don't have something, God is withholding it from us for our good.

How would your life and attitude change if you spent less time comparing yourself and your situation to others, and more time being grateful for what you have and who God has made you to be?

...you into a new person by changing the way you think. Then you will learn to know God's will for you, which is good and pleasing and perfect. Don't copy the behavior and customs of this world, but let God transform

Take a good look at all the gifts God has given you. Write or draw 3-5 things you're thankful for.

Romans 12:2

CONQUERING THE IF ONLYS ...

It's tempting to think that if one or two things in our lives were different, then we would be content. It's what I call the if-onlys. *If only I had made the musical, then I would feel better about myself. If only he would ask me to the dance, then I would fit in with the popular crowd. If only I had a bigger house, then I could have friends over and not be embarrassed.*

There is just one problem with that line of thought: if you aren't happy now, you won't be happy if your circumstances change. If you aren't content now, then even if you get what you want, you'll just find a new reason to be discontent.

There was a woman in the Bible named Hannah, and what she wanted most in the world was a baby. Year after year she watched her friends have babies, while she was still barren. She poured out her heart to God in anger and frustration, and then the Bible says that after she prayed, she wiped away her tears and went away happy (1 Samuel 1:18). She still didn't have what she wanted, but she chose to live in hope that God would be good to her.

You can do that too. Whether or not your circumstances change, you can be filled with joy and peace through the power of the Holy Spirit (Romans 15:13). Place your hope not in what you have or what you lack, but in God—the source of true hope.

I pray that God, the source of hope, will fill you completely with joy and peace because you trust in him. Then you will overflow with confident hope through the power of the Holy Spirit.

Romans 15:13

Fill the space above with doodles of all the ways God gives you joy and peace even while you're still waiting for the answers to your deepest prayers.

Week

5

Family Matters

HONOR OR NOT?

It was many years ago, but I remember it like it was yesterday. I slammed the door and threw the book I was holding across the room. *Why does it have to be so hard to get along with Mom? Her rules just don't seem fair.*

And then I heard a little voice in my head—not a creepy, maybe-you-belong-in-a-hospital kind of voice, but an internal whisper: "Honor your father and mother. Then you will live a long, full life in the land the Lord your God is giving you" (Exodus 20:12). I hadn't been doing that very well lately. It seemed like we were arguing about everything and nothing. Maybe it was time to try a different approach.

That night I prayed that God would help me honor my parents. The next day I looked for things I could agree with my mom about. I found a few nice things to say to her. The day after that I did the same thing, and it got a little easier. Over time, our relationship improved—and when it did, she was able to give me a little more freedom. I wish I had decided to try doing things God's way earlier! He really does know best, and honoring your parents pays off in the end.

Honor your father and mother.
Then you will live a long, full life in the land the
LORD your God is giving you.

Exodus 20:12

_____

_____

_____

_____

_____

_____

_____

_____

_____

Write your mom or dad a letter, telling them
all the ways you wish your relationship was better.
This is just for you — you don't have to show it to
anybody. But maybe after you write your thoughts
here you'd like to write a real letter to your mom
or dad that honors them for all the good
things they bring to your life.

RIVAL OR FRIEND?

Do you have a younger brother or sister, someone who came after you and stole all the attention? Do people call them "cute" and let them get away with things while you get blamed for their mischief? Do they sneak into your room and steal your stuff—and then wreck it? The only thing harder to live with than a younger sibling is an older sibling who gets to do everything first. . . .

Let's face it, living in a family is hard, and they don't call it sibling rivalry for nothing. But let me tell you a secret: a little effort on your part can turn your siblings into friends! Think how much better life would be if you and your brothers and sisters enjoyed one another rather than fighting. You could have built-in playmates and confidants. All it takes is you making a first step. Maybe you can invite your little brother to play a game with you or paint your little sister's nails. Ask your older sister if you can help clean her room, or your big brother if you can hang out—without being annoying.

If you think about it, loving your brothers and sisters is a great way to obey God's command to love others. Besides, the Bible says that if we can't love the people around us, we probably aren't doing a very good job of loving God, either.

If we don't love people we can see, how can we love God, whom we cannot see? 1 John 4:20

In the space above, draw a picture of you and your siblings. Then doodle some ways you can build a better relationship with them.

POSITIONED FOR A PURPOSE

Yesterday we talked about how your siblings can become your friends if you want them to. But there is more. God didn't place you in your family, and in your position in that family, by accident. Just like everything else, He carefully placed you exactly where you are for a reason.

If you have younger brothers and sisters, they are a built-in opportunity for you to become a leader. They automatically look up to you (even if they would never admit that), and they are watching your every move. You can use your position to help them learn more about God and His love and learn to make good decisions. Younger siblings can do this for their older siblings, too. The Bible tells us not to let people look down on us because we're young, but to set an example (1 Timothy 4:12). Whether you are the youngest or the oldest or somewhere in between, look for opportunities. Take your brother or sister out for ice cream and ask them what they like or don't like about church. Or even read the Bible and pray with them.

If you're an only child, that's an opportunity, too. You can reach out to your friends and have them over, like surrogate siblings. Especially look for people who seem to have a tough home life. Maybe spending time with you and your parents in a happy home is just what they need to help them believe that maybe God really does love them.

Make the most of *every opportunity* in these EVIL DAYS.

EPHESIANS 5:16

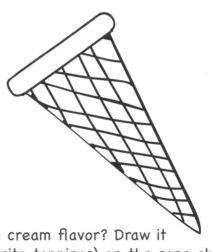

What's your favorite ice cream flavor? Draw it
(and don't forget to add your favorite toppings) on the cone above.
Now think of someone you can take out for ice cream just for fun,
and maybe also to help them take the next step in their walk
with God. Is it a sibling? A friend? Even a parent? Make a date!

WHEN HOME IS A BATTLEGROUND

God designed the home to be a place of comfort and security, the place where we learn that we are loved so we can go out into the world and achieve our purpose. His purpose is for families to provide stability and unconditional love.

Sadly, some homes resemble battlegrounds more than cozy dwellings. The parents fight, hurling angry words and harsh criticisms at one another. They belittle their children and are so wrapped up in their own problems that they don't show love. Or maybe it's worse than that, and they abuse their children. If you are being abused, or even if you wonder if you are, stop reading and go tell someone—a pastor, teacher, or a friend's parent. Your abuser loses his or her power when you speak out.

If your home is a battleground, you are not alone. God sees, He knows, and He cares. He is with you always—every time you feel hurt and alone, every time you are huddled up crying because you just can't take it anymore. In fact, the Bible tells us that He catches every tear you cry and holds it in a bottle (Psalm 56:8) and that He is especially close to the brokenhearted (Psalm 34:18). What happens in your home is not your fault, and God is right beside you in your darkest moments, loving you and telling you that you are important to Him. Cling to that truth, believe it, and turn to Him for comfort and help.

The LORD is my light and my salvation –
so why should I be afraid? The LORD is my
fortress, protecting me from danger,
so why should I tremble?

Psalm 27:1

Imagine yourself in a
cozy, safe place like
the bed pictured here.
Doodle about what
things help you feel safe, and
then pray and thank God that
He is your fortress, protecting
you from danger.

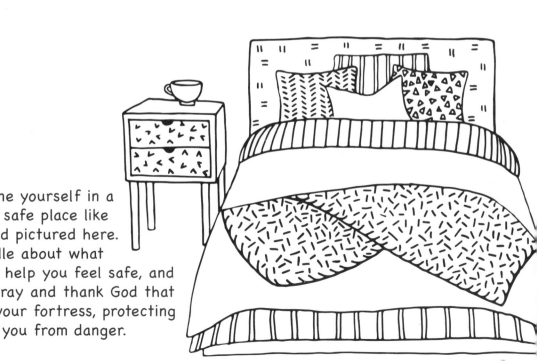

THE PERFECT FATHER

What is your dad like? Is he tall? Funny? Totally embarrassing? Does he like spicy food or chocolate cake better? Is he one of your favorite people, or are you a little bit afraid of him?

Some of us have terrific dads, and some of us have really awful ones. Perhaps you don't even know who your dad is. But here is what we have in common: every single one of us will be disappointed by our earthly fathers. That's because they are all sinners. They may not intend to hurt us, but at some point they will.

The good news is that all of us have something else in common: we have a perfect heavenly Father. Whatever is great about your dad, God is ALL that, only better. And whatever is awful about your dad, God isn't that at all. The Bible tells us that God loves us unconditionally, that He is always there for us, and that He is our strength when we are weak. If you have a hard time believing that God your Father loves you and is working out a good plan in your life because your earthly dad fell so far short, find a trusted pastor or counselor and ask them for perspective. It's really important that we understand what a great Father God is, because it affects everything else about our walk with Him. The reason we can trust God in every circumstance is because He is the perfect heavenly Father.

The LORD is like a
father to his children,
tender and compassionate
to those who fear him.

Psalm 103:13

Think about everything you wish your dad was, or what a dad
should be, and write those things down above. For instance, by his
hand you might write: "Picks me up when I fall." Thank God that He
is your perfect heavenly Father who does everything for you
that a good earthly father does—only more and better.

Week
6

Friends and Foes

CHOOSE WISELY

If you're like me, your favorite thing to do is hang out with your BFF. She's the one person you can relax and be yourself around, and she loves you no matter what. She just gets you—in all your weird wonderfulness—and you know that she's always got your back. Or at least that's how it *should* be.

Whether we like it or not, who we hang out with changes who we are. If you want to see what you're becoming, take a good look at your best friends. Do you like what you see? Are they helping you grow closer to God? Or do you seem to be getting in trouble a lot more often than you used to? Are they encouraging and loyal, or are they fair-weather friends?

Proverbs tells us, "As iron sharpens iron, so a friend sharpens a friend" (Proverbs 27:17). In other words, friends are supposed to make us a better person and help us make good choices. They should always be there for us and want good things for us. And they should challenge us in good ways. If your friends aren't like that, it might be time to find some new friends.

Walk with the wise and become wise; associate with fools and get in trouble.

Proverbs 13:20

Who's your BFF? Think about the last time you hung out together. Is she helping you become wise, or is she causing you to act like a fool? Write down some of your thoughts above. If your best friends are not leading you in a good direction, think of some people you know who might be better friends for you, and jot down some ways you could develop those friendships.

FRIENDS AND FRENEMIES

What was the last thing you and your good friends fought about? Was it over what to do together, or who to do it with? Was it over a boy (totally not worth it!)? Even if you have the most wonderful friends in the world, at some point you will have conflict. One of you will say or do the wrong thing, the other person will get offended, and the next thing you know it feels like your whole world is imploding.

That's why the most important thing in every relationship, including friendship, is forgiveness. We need to get really good at asking for forgiveness—using real words, not just brushing things under the rug—and offering forgiveness, even when it's not asked for. Holding on to an offense is like drinking poison and hoping the other person dies. In the end, bitterness only hurts you.

If you're tired of all the drama, here are some steps to take: 1) Stop talking and really listen to understand the other person's point of view. 2) Don't say things in the heat of the moment that you won't mean later (no gossip!). 3) Be a peacemaker, turning away wrath with a gentle answer rather than trying to prove your point. 4) Forgive, forgive, and forgive some more. Let go of your anger and ask God to heal your hurt from the inside out.

A gentle answer deflects anger,
but harsh words make tempers flare.
PROVERBS 15:1

When we're angry,
we have a tendency to
forget about the good things
we love about our friends and
focus on their faults. Doodle about
some happy memories you have
with your friends, or some ideas
for fun things you'd like to do
together in the future.

MEAN GIRLS

Mean Girls was a funny movie back in 2004, but mean girls in real life are not so funny. They are the cliquey cool girls, the ones who love to be mean. When they set their sights on a new victim, they will stop at nothing to make her life miserable—perhaps you know that firsthand.

So what are we supposed to do with the mean girls in our lives, especially if we find ourselves at the receiving end of their taunts? The Bible would call these people our enemies, and it has a lot to say about them. In fact, Jesus said, "Love your enemies! Pray for those who persecute you! In that way, you will be acting as true children of your Father in heaven" (Matthew 5:44–45). In another place it says to do good to our enemies and lend to them without expecting anything back (Luke 6:35).

Now, that doesn't mean we have to like the mean girls or excuse their behavior. But when someone mistreats us, we can love them back with Christ's love. We are powerless to love them on our own, but we can love them with the power of the Holy Spirit. Imagine yourself as the pipeline through which Jesus' love flows. But don't miss that second part of Jesus' command, to pray for them. It's funny how when we start to pray for someone, we find it impossible to hate them. Prayer is like our secret weapon for loving our enemies.

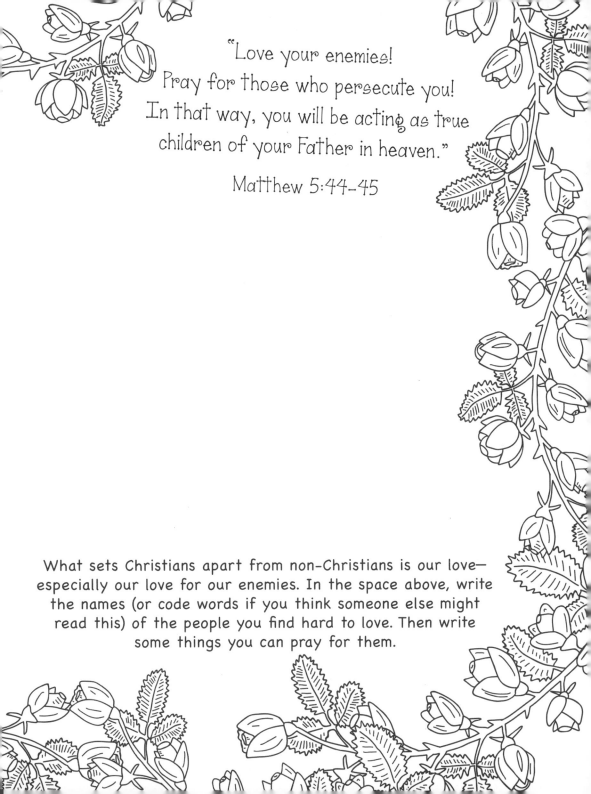

"Love your enemies!
Pray for those who persecute you!
In that way, you will be acting as true
children of your Father in heaven."

Matthew 5:44-45

What sets Christians apart from non-Christians is our love—
especially our love for our enemies. In the space above, write
the names (or code words if you think someone else might
read this) of the people you find hard to love. Then write
some things you can pray for them.

BE THE NOTICER

Whether you call it a squad or a team or something else, it's nice to have a group you belong to. We all long to fit in and have a gang to be a part of—our *people*. But have you ever noticed that some girls don't seem to have a group? They sit alone at the lunch table. They hang out on the edges of the youth group. They are awkward and hard to talk to. They just don't quite fit in.

As Christians, it's our job to offer them the gift of friendship—even if it hurts our social standing, even if it's hard, and even if we really don't want to do it. That's part of loving our neighbor as ourselves, the commandment that comes second only to loving God before anything else. And guess what? Loving the people around us is a way we show love to God, since that's what He does. So really you're killing two birds with one stone.

Now, as you're reading this, I bet someone is coming to mind. You can picture her right now, and you're getting uncomfortable because you really don't want God to ask you to be nice to her. That's the girl you need to reach out to—tomorrow. You will never know what a huge difference it could make to her when you just offer to sit by her, or hang out, or give her a ride to youth group.

Dear friends, let us continue to *love* one another, for love comes from God. ANYONE WHO LOVES IS A *child of God* and knows God.

1 John 4:7

Ask God to show you who the person is who needs a friend, and then doodle some ways you can be a friend to them. Don't let them sit alone at the lunch table one more day.

THE FRIEND WHO STICKS CLOSER THAN A BROTHER

We've been talking about friends this week, and how to pick good ones and stay friends with them through thick and thin. But the fact is, our friends will disappoint us. They are sinners, just like we are, and at some point along the way they will hurt us and we will hurt them. It's just a part of life.

That's why it's so important to know the One who will always be our friend—Jesus. Proverbs calls Him the friend who sticks closer than a brother (Proverbs 18:24). He will always love us, will never fail us, and is always working for our good. He will never let us down. And He will always be there to listen and comfort us when we are hurting, even if it's the middle of the night. With Jesus, we never have to be afraid that He will change His mind about us or suddenly decide He doesn't like us. Jesus is our ever-faithful, always-patient, unconditionally-loving friend.

Do you know Jesus as that kind of friend? If you don't, pray and ask Him to show you how much He loves you. Tell Him you want to be His friend—He will always answer that prayer! In fact, He's been waiting for you to say that to Him.

[Jesus said,] "You are my friends if you do what I command. I no longer call you slaves, because a master doesn't confide in his slaves. Now you are my friends, since I have told you everything the Father told me."

John 15:14-15

BFFs

In the space above, write a love note to Jesus, thanking Him for always being your friend and sticking closer than a brother.

Week

7

True Love

BOYFRIENDS AND BOY FRIENDS

Who was your best friend when you were younger? Maybe it was a boy—when we're little, girls often have lots of friends who are boys. But then we get older and things get . . . complicated. Boys start to act weird. We think they are a friend, and then they decide to ask us out, and suddenly everything is AWKWARD. Or we decide we like them, and then *we're* all kinds of awkward.

What's a girl to do? Well, being friends with boys is hard. But that doesn't mean it's impossible, and the perspective that boys offer and the fun they bring to life is worth the complications of opposite-sex friendship. The trick is to treat every boy like a brother—and if they're Christians, that is really what they are because they are a brother in Christ. What does that mean? Be kind. Look out for their best interests. Protect their feelings. And perhaps most importantly of all, don't be more friendly with them than you would be with a brother. Don't over-share or give too much physical contact. Keep your boy friends in the friend zone.

What about when you decide you'd like them to be a boyfriend rather than a boy friend? Well, we'll get to that tomorrow.

A friend is always loyal, and a brother is born to help in time of need. Proverbs 17:17

Write down all the things you love about having boys as friends—and maybe jot down some guys' names you haven't seen in a while and set up a time to get together with them.

PUPPY LOVE AND INFATUATION

You're walking along, minding your own business, and then suddenly the boys you've known since kindergarten seem, well, different. They are cute. And you can imagine yourself as a Disney princess dancing the night away in his arms. Well, maybe not that. But all the same, the boys who have always had cooties turn into prince charming seemingly overnight.

It's hard to know what to do with all the feelings and the crushes and the hormones. Your parents may call it puppy love, but a new crush pretty much dominates your thought life for a few weeks—or longer. And there's nothing wrong with that. But it is important to keep your feet on the ground even if your head and heart are in the clouds.

Perspective. That's what you need when it comes to crushes and infatuation. You can enjoy all the fun of romance, but it's important to remember that chances are good that this boy you like today won't be your final true love. And when you do find your final true love, you're going to want to have saved your tenderest words and kisses for him. Besides, even if this boy turns out to be THE ONE, you have lots of time before you're ready to get married. So take it slow, enjoy the romance, but don't push things too fast.

Promise me, O women of Jerusalem, not to
awaken love until the time is right.

Song of Solomon 8:4

When we're crushing on someone, it's easy to get carried away.
In the space above, jot down some verses that might help you have
patience. Here are some ideas to get you started: 2 Timothy 2:22;
1 Timothy 4:12; Proverbs 4:23; Jeremiah 17:9. What are some
practical ways you can keep your runaway feelings in check?

BUILDING FOR THE FUTURE

There will come a time—and maybe it's already here—when you are considering whether or not to date someone. It's easy to be swayed by the wonderful feeling of being with a boy, of holding hands and feeling like you belong together. But before you get carried away, there are some important things to consider.

You see, dating is eventually supposed to lead to marriage. Any relationship that doesn't lead to marriage will lead to a breakup, which usually involves tears and a pint of Ben & Jerry's ice cream. So be careful whom you date. Could you maybe see yourself marrying this person? If not, then you shouldn't be dating him.

The best time to think about what kind of person you want to date and eventually marry is before you are feeling all warm and fuzzy toward the cute boy in your first-period class. For sure he should be a Christian (read 2 Corinthians 6:14 to see why); kind to everyone; encouraging (the kind of person who helps you be your best self); honest; and faithful. Then there are characteristics that would make a boy fit well with your personality. Do you want him to have a sense of humor or be a little more serious? Be more organized or spontaneous? Be sporty or bookish? It's both useful and fun to think about these things even if you haven't found THE ONE yet.

We *love* each other because he loved us first.

1 John 4:19

The best summary of what a healthy, loving relationship looks like is found in 1 Corinthians 13:4-7. Read what that says, and then doodle some ideas of what your ideal boyfriend would be like.

PURITY

We can't talk about boys without touching on the topic of purity. God designed men and women to fall in love and eventually have children. That's right—God invented sex. And the Bible tells us that sex is a good gift, one that in some mysterious way reflects who God is.

There is a catch: sex is only good within the boundary God set for it, which is marriage. We are to be joined together in the lifelong covenant of marriage before we enjoy the gift of sex. And the ironic thing is that when people take that boundary away from sex and are intimate with people before marriage, they actually ruin the gift for themselves. They will have to live with the consequences of their choice forever, and in the case of sex before marriage it is a gift that hurts the woman and her future husband most of all.

Now, marriage is a long way off for most of you reading this book. So that means you need to set boundaries around your relationships and your body to protect the gift of sex and save it for marriage so it can be the best it can be. The secret is to set boundaries long before you are tempted to have sex. Don't be alone in the house with a boy. Don't get carried away with kissing. Treat each other in such a way that you will never have regrets, even if you end up marrying someone else.

And so, dear brothers and sisters, I plead with you to give your bodies to God because of all he has done for you. Let them be a living and holy sacrifice — the kind he will find acceptable. This is truly the way to worship him. Romans 12:1

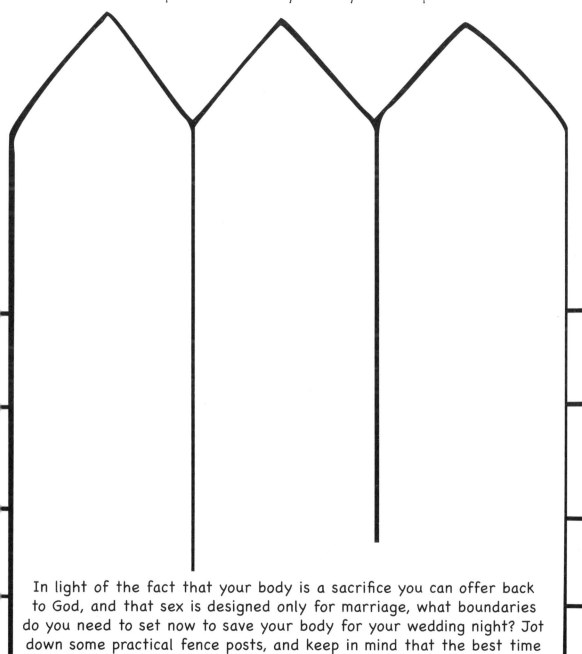

In light of the fact that your body is a sacrifice you can offer back to God, and that sex is designed only for marriage, what boundaries do you need to set now to save your body for your wedding night? Jot down some practical fence posts, and keep in mind that the best time to talk with your boyfriend about this is before a romantic moment.

MODESTY

The experts tell us that boys are more visual than girls are. In other words, when women dress in a way that calls attention to the parts of their body that should be covered up in front of everyone except their husband, men are sometimes tempted by thoughts that they should only be thinking about their wives. Like we said yesterday, sex is a good gift that is only to be enjoyed within the boundaries of marriage.

Where does that leave us as young women who want to look our best? Well, it's not up to you to make sure that boys don't think lustful thoughts, but it is up to you to treat them like you would a brother. That means that you should make it easier (rather than harder) for them to remain pure in their thought life. Choose fashions that cover you appropriately—and that includes avoiding things that are too tight. If you're wearing leggings, it's probably best to have on a long top that hits you somewhere on your thighs. If your top is see-through, wear a tank under it. Be sensible.

Really, dressing modestly is a way of valuing ourselves. When we dress in a way that shows us to be intelligent, capable young women, others will treat us that way. On the other hand, if we show off our bodies to gain the attention of boys, we will probably gain the wrong kind of attention.

I want women to be modest in their appearance. They should wear decent and appropriate clothing and not draw attention to themselves by the way they fix their hair or by wearing gold or pearls or expensive clothes.

1 Timothy 2:9

Fashion can be fun! Doodle some of your favorite looks, and as you do so, think about whether the way you dress is "decent and appropriate" like the Scripture verse above commands.

Week

8

True Beauty

BEAUTY IN THE BROKEN

There is an ancient Japanese art form called Kintsugi in which broken pottery is repaired with gold. Rather than hiding the cracks and breaks, the artist calls attention to them by filling them with precious gold. The brokenness is used and adorned, taking an ordinary piece of pottery and turning it into something of greater value and beauty. The end result is a vessel veined with pure gold, tiny lines carefully repaired and strengthened and beautified.

That's kind of like what God does with the brokenness in our lives. He tenderly cares for our places of hurt and makes them even stronger than before. I imagine Him bending down, gold-covered paintbrush in hand, and caring for each miniscule crack in me— every place someone has wounded me with their words, every difficult experience, and even the cracks I caused myself through foolish and sinful choices.

God is in the business of restoration and healing. He brings beauty from the ashes of our suffering. He binds up our wounds and comforts us, and then uses the broken places we thought we should hide as experiences that we can use to comfort others. No pain in our lives is wasted when we offer it back to God and ask Him to heal us and use our suffering for His glory.

He comforts us in all our troubles
so that we can comfort others. When they are
troubled, we will be able to give them the
same comfort God has given us.

2 Corinthians 1:4

Think about the places of brokenness in your life, the things
that you would rather hide. As you decorate this tea cup, include
some cracks filled with gold. Pray and ask God to heal the cracks in
your life, make them beautiful, and then use you to help
others who are struggling in similar ways.

THE RIGHT LOOK

Let's be honest here: how much time do you spend getting ready in the morning, or for a night out? How much time do you spend each day in God's Word, learning what He wants you to look like?

There is nothing wrong with learning fun new ways to style your hair or put on makeup. God likes beauty, and He designed us to enjoy creativity and beauty. In fact, He wants you to see yourself as the beautiful creature He sees when He looks at you.

But there is something wrong with focusing too much on how we look on the outside, especially if we neglect our inner beauty. It matters more that you are a kind person than that you know how to put together the perfect outfit. It matters more that you know how much God loves you than that you know the latest hairstyle trend. In fact, if you wake up late and only have time for one thing, it's probably more important to spend a few minutes reading your Bible than brushing your hair!

Don't be concerned about the outward beauty of fancy
hairstyles, expensive jewelry, or beautiful clothes. You should
clothe yourselves instead with the beauty that comes from within,
the unfading beauty of a gentle and quiet spirit,
which is so precious to God.

I Peter 3:3-4

How is your inward adornment? On the bottles above,
write some character traits you need more of, and then
ask God to help you develop those.

A GENTLE AND QUIET SPIRIT

The world can be divided into two types of people: the talkers and the listeners. Psychologists call them extroverts and introverts. Which one are you? Do you think things through by talking, or do you prefer to only speak when you've had time to think about what you're going to say? Do you sometimes wonder if you've said too much, or do people often ask you what you're thinking about? Would you rather go to a party, or stay home and read a good book?

Regardless of whether we are talkers or listeners (and the world needs both—that's why God made us all different!), the Bible tells us that each of us needs to develop a gentle and quiet spirit. It's not about *how much* we talk but rather *the way* we talk. We can think of it as a sense of settled peace that spills over and helps others feel more at peace. It's like the difference between feeling chaotic and snapping at people, versus feeling content inside so that you can focus on the needs of others.

The best way to develop a gentle and quiet spirit is—you guessed it—spending time with God. When we know how loved we are and trust that God is in control and is working everything for our good, we will feel settled inside. And when we're settled inside, we can be gentle toward others.

Clothe yourselves instead with the beauty that comes from within, the unfading beauty of a gentle and quiet spirit, which is so precious to God.

I Peter 3:4

We can think of the gentle and quiet spirit God wants us
to have like clothes that we put on each day. We might not wake
up feeling gentle and quiet on the inside, but with God's help we can
refocus ourselves on what really matters and get ready to greet the day
with a settled mind and heart. As you color this closet full of clothes in
your favorite colors and designs, ask God to help you clothe
yourself in the beauty that comes from within.

BODY PARTS

Let me tell you a little secret: every woman on the planet has a "problem" body part, something she believes isn't her best asset and tries to cover up. For some of us it's that our hips are too big, and every piece of chocolate cake seems to go straight there. For others it's a prominent nose or big feet—but trust me when I say that everybody has some body part they don't like.

I don't think that's a bad thing, because it helps us understand the body of Christ better. All Christians together make up the body of Christ. When we work together, using the gifts God has given us, we can do great things. The key is that we all have to do our little part and let everybody else do their little part. Some people kind of stick out, like a big nose, and some people are hidden, like pinky toes, but if you've ever broken your pinky toe you know how important those people are!

In the church, we need every single person and the gifts they have to offer. We especially need the people who do the less visible or lower-status jobs. So next time you bemoan your least favorite body part, offer a prayer of thanks for all the people who make your church effective, especially those who do the hidden jobs like taking out the trash. Then think about whether or not you're doing your part to build up the body of Christ.

The human body has many parts, but the many parts make up one whole body. So it is with the body of Christ.... If the whole body were an eye, how would you hear? Or if your whole body were an ear, how would you smell anything? But our bodies have many parts, and God has put each part just where he wants it.

I Corinthians
12:12, 17–18

On the body above, write in some of the gifts God has given the church, and maybe even jot down the names of some of your friends next to the body part they represent. For instance, next to the hand you might write: "Meeting people's needs" or next to the heart you might write: "Loving those who are different with the love of Christ."

Distorted Mirrors

Have you ever been in a store dressing room and thought you looked totally awesome in a new outfit, and then brought it home and it didn't look as good? Or have you ever tried something on in the store and thought it looked terrible, and then realized that the mirror was distorting your body and the lighting was making your skin look yellow? Some stores really aren't doing themselves any favors by using poor-quality mirrors and dim lighting in the dressing rooms.

The way we talk to or about ourselves is kind of like a mirror. Sometimes we say true things: "God made me just the way I am for a purpose, and He loves me more than I can ever know!" But sometimes we say not-true things, perhaps repeating lies someone else has said about us: "I can never do this. I'm so ugly. I'm worthless." It's like we're holding up a distorted mirror and believing that we are seeing the truth about who we are.

The messages we say and believe about ourselves are what psychologists call self-talk. Our self-talk greatly affects what we think about ourselves, what we do, and even what we attempt to do. So it's really important to say true things about ourselves, and the voice we need to put in our heads is the voice of truth: God's voice, which we can hear in the Bible.

Ephesians 2:10   Psalm 139:14   Genesis 1:27
Romans 12:6   1 Thessalonians 1:4

Look up these verses and write down on the
mirror above what God says about you.

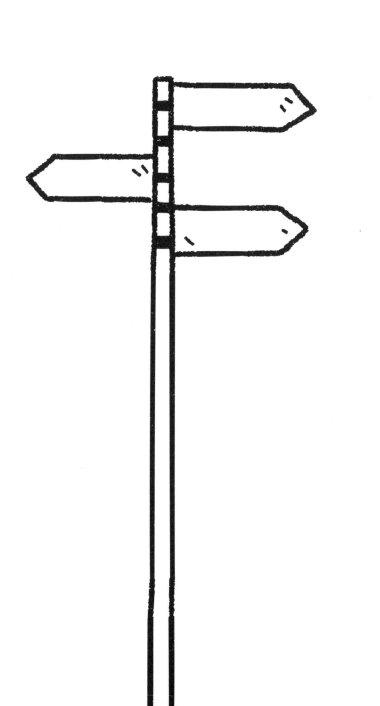

Week

9

Choices, Choices

WHAT'S IN YOUR HAND?

Cell phones. Can't live with 'em, can't live without 'em. Are your parents always on your back about how much time you spend on your phone? Are your friends always complaining that you don't get back to them fast enough when they send you a message? Do you sometimes annoy *yourself* by how you use your phone?

Technology is a tricky thing. Experts tell us that as we use our phones, we actually rewire our brains to need them more. It's almost like a drug in its addictiveness. What does God think about phones? Well, they certainly can be a good tool to stay in touch with people. You can even read your Bible on your phone!

But too much of a good thing can be a bad thing. The apostle Paul wrote, "Fix your thoughts on what is true, and honorable, and right, and pure, and lovely, and admirable. Think about things that are excellent and worthy of praise" (Philippians 4:8). That's a good test for how you should use your phone. If it's helping you fix your eyes on true and honorable and pure things, then you're using it as a helpful tool. If it's dragging you into grey areas or simply sucking too many hours out of your day, maybe it's time to reevaluate and set some boundaries for yourself.

All right, it's time to get real here. How much time did you spend staring at your phone today? If you're being honest, the answer is probably higher than it should be. Use the space on the cell phone above to write some rules for yourself that will help you use your phone as a helpful tool to focus on what's truly important. In our house, it seems to help a lot if we only use our phones in public areas (not in bedrooms) and turn them off at 9:30 PM.

UNDER PRESSURE

I never meant for it to happen . . . it's just that my friends pressured me day after day, until finally I gave in. And now I regret it. Have you ever felt like that, or made decisions you weren't comfortable with to make your friends happy?

It's hard to stand up to temptation, especially when it comes from our friends—and when not giving in is social suicide. The good news is that God has promised to always provide a way out from temptation. First Corinthians 10:13 says, "When you are tempted, he will show you a way out so that you can endure." No matter what we are tempted to do, God has promised to provide a way for us to do what is right—and it's always worth it to do things God's way, even if some of our so-called friends reject us because of it.

On the flip side, peer pressure can be used for good. Hebrews 10:24 says, "Let us think of ways to motivate one another to acts of love and good works." Imagine what would happen if you and your Christian friends decided to find creative ways to remind one another to do acts of love and good works. Maybe you can start a text or chat group to share encouraging Bible verses, or brainstorm some service projects you can do together.

The temptations in your life are no different from what others experience. And God is faithful. He will not allow the temptation to be more than you can stand. When you are tempted, he will show you a way out so that you can endure.

1 Corinthians 10:13

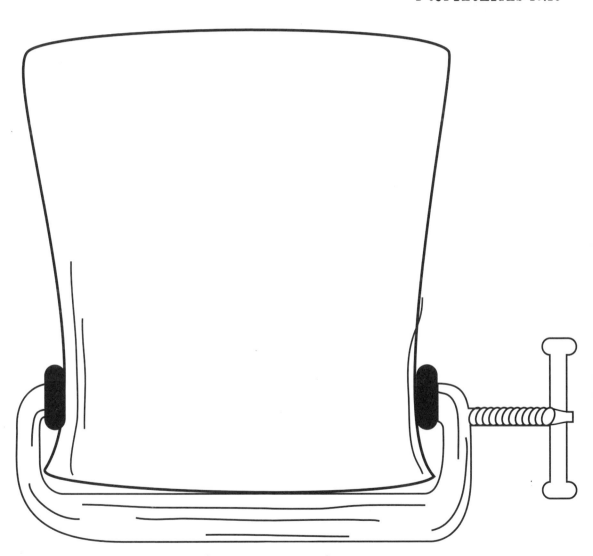

What kinds of things do you feel pressure to do?
Make a list of things you're tempted by in the vise above. Then draw arrows and brainstorm ways you can get out of those temptations.

WHAT'S THAT YOU SAY?

One of my favorite group games is called telephone Pictionary. Everybody starts by writing a sentence on a slip of paper. The next person in the circle takes another piece of paper and draws a picture to illustrate that sentence. The next person in the circle looks at the picture and writes a sentence, and so on, alternating between pictures and words. At the end you have a stack of paper. The bottom one has the original sentence, and then you can trace the "logic" that got you to the final sentence and picture.

It's a hilarious game, and it illustrates well what happens when we spread gossip—only the results of gossip are not usually funny at all. When we share someone else's secrets or tell other people what so-and-so said, we often get the story just a little bit wrong. As the story spreads, a few more details get confused. In the end, the story bears little to no resemblance to what actually happened.

Even worse, we often hurt people along the way. The best strategy is not to say something about someone else that you haven't been given permission to share, and to never say something behind someone's back that you wouldn't say to their face. Before you speak, ask yourself some simple questions: Is this true? Is it necessary for me to say it? Is it kind? And most important of all, should I be talking *with* the person instead of *about* them?

A TROUBLEMAKER

plants seeds of strife; gossip separates
the best of *friends.*

Proverbs 16:28

In the space, write out some questions that
can help you decide whether or not to share
information about someone else. Ask God to
help you be self-controlled in what you say.

FINDING GOD'S WILL

What do you want to be when you grow up? Lots of young people seem to want to be a teacher, doctor, or engineer. Do you love to think about what you might do someday, or does it stress you out? The older we get, the more we start to wonder what God's will for us is. It can be a little scary, actually. Fortunately, God's will is a lot simpler than finding a particular career or calling.

God's will is less about what job we will have someday and more about whether or not we obey Him. It's less about career and more about character. It is about habit and lifestyle, not livelihood. In fact, every time the Bible mentions God's will it's talking about obedience—things like loving others, doing what is right, and seeking justice for those who are being mistreated. Those are things you can do right now, long before you have a career.

Today, as you go to school or hang out with friends, think about ways you can fulfill God's will. How can you be kind to others? How can you speak truth and stand up for people who can't stand up for themselves? How can you be like Jesus to those around you?

Don't copy the behavior and customs of this world, but let God transform you into a new person by changing the way you think. Then you will learn to know God's will for you, which is good and pleasing and perfect.

Romans 12:2

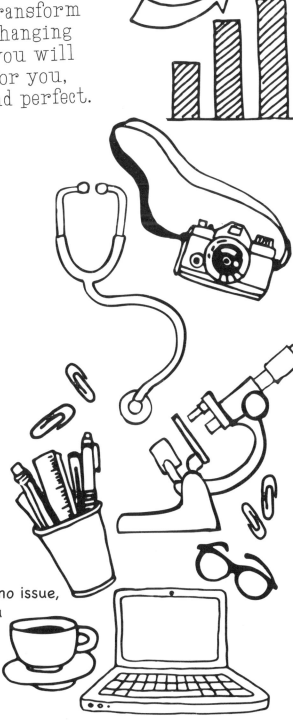

If money, education, and time were no issue, what would you like to do when you grow up? Draw pictures and doodle your wildest dreams. Then ask God to help you do His will wherever you are now and wherever you end up, every day of your life.

A LITTLE PIECE OF QUIET

We've been talking a lot in this book about spending time with God, and as you've been going through this devotional, you've been doing just that! But it's good to have a plan for building a daily quiet time into your schedule. Relationships don't just happen, they take some time and effort—and it's no different in our relationship with God. If we think we can just go to church on Sundays and call it good, we won't grow much in our relationship with Him, and we'll be missing out.

Lots of people decide to read through the Bible, which is a great thing. But if you start in Genesis you might give up by the time you reach the Book of Numbers, which is basically long lists of names, or Leviticus and Deuteronomy, which contain a lot of laws and regulations that don't apply to us anymore now that Jesus has come and brought the new covenant.

So here are some ideas: start with the gospels and learn about Jesus. Read the Bible in smaller chunks so you don't get too overwhelmed. Find someone else who wants to read the Bible and check in with each other to make sure you're really doing it. Install a Bible app on your phone that will give you some Bible verses to read every day. Look for an engaging devotional to read after you're done with this one. Ask your Sunday school teacher or youth leader for more ideas on how to spend regular time in God's Word.

All Scripture is inspired by God and is useful to teach us what is true and to make us realize what is wrong in our lives. It corrects us when we are wrong and teaches us to do what is right. 2 Timothy 3:16

It's time to make a plan. How are you going to schedule a daily quiet time into your busy life? In the space above, jot down a plan. Where will you do it? What time each day? What Bible-reading plan are you going to follow? How will you mix it up to keep it interesting?

Week

10

Prayer

WHAT IS PRAYER, AND WHY SHOULD I DO IT?

What would you do if the secretary of state came and told you that the president had invited you to the Oval Office to give your advice on some important issues? I don't know about you, but if I heard that I could go and talk to the president of the United States and have influence over important decisions, I would definitely go.

That's kind of what prayer is, except it is so much more than that because God is so much greater than any president. In its most basic form, prayer is talking to God. It may include everything from shouts of praise to silent meditation on Scripture—and everything in between. You can use formal prayers that you find in a book or make up your own. It can be an organized prayer time or a quick plea of "Help me, God!" Whatever form it takes, you have the immense privilege of talking directly to the Creator of the universe and knowing that He hears you and He cares about what you say.

Really, that last sentence answers the why question: Why pray? Because you can! The Bible describes prayer as going into the most holy place, the very throne room of God, and sitting on His lap because He's your Father. It also says that Jesus prays for us: "Therefore he [Jesus] is able, once and forever, to save those who come to God through him. He lives forever to intercede with God on their behalf" (Hebrews 7:25).

And so, dear brothers and sisters, we can boldly enter heaven's Most Holy Place because of the blood of Jesus ... Let us go right into the presence of God with sincere hearts fully trusting him. For our guilty consciences have been sprinkled with Christ's blood to make us clean, and our bodies have been washed with pure water.

HEBREWS 10:19, 22

Close your eyes and imagine yourself going boldly into the throne room of God. Color the picture using some of the images you see when you imagine being in the presence of God. You can find a description of God's throne room in Revelation 4.

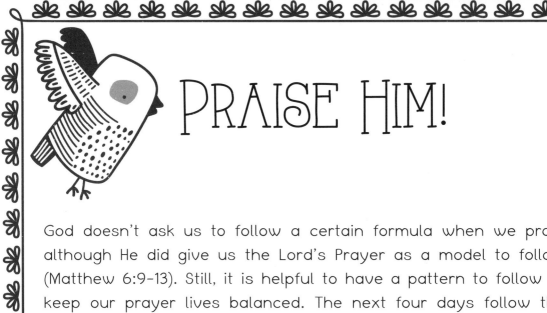

PRAISE HIM!

God doesn't ask us to follow a certain formula when we pray, although He did give us the Lord's Prayer as a model to follow (Matthew 6:9-13). Still, it is helpful to have a pattern to follow to keep our prayer lives balanced. The next four days follow the acronym PRAY: Praise, Repent, Ask, and Yield.

Prayer should always begin and end with praise. We pray because of who God is. If He weren't all-powerful and all-knowing, there would be no point in prayer. If He weren't good and perfect and loving, we wouldn't be allowed to pray. But because God is all of those things and more, we can approach Him and tell Him what we think and feel.

If you're feeling low and can't immediately think of things to praise God for, open up your Bible. On every page you can find something to thank Him for. He is just, holy, merciful, beautiful, and powerful. You can also use the words of a song to praise Him. If you think through your day, even if it's been a horrible no-good very-bad day, you can find even more things to praise and thank God for. If nothing else, He woke you up this morning and you will be able to go to bed tonight. The main thing is to honor God for who He is and what He has done.

Let all that I am **praise THE LORD;** may I never forget the *good things* he does for me.

PSALM 103:2

In the space above, doodle some things you praise God for. You can find some lists of God's praiseworthy attributes at Psalm 103 or Ephesians 1:3–11.

REPENT
OF YOUR SINS

Have you ever said something or done something and then instantly regretted it? Maybe you blurted out an angry response without thinking or called someone a name. Maybe you lied or gossiped, and you wish you could take it back but the relationship is already ruined beyond repair. Every one of us has done things we wish we could un-do.

After we've praised God for who He is, the next thing we need to do when we pray is repent of our sin. It's an amazing thing that God invites us to come to Him with all of our sins, all of our failures, and all of our regrets. More amazing still is that when we confess our sins, God graciously forgives. He gives us a fresh start and erases our sin. He casts our sin away as far as the east is from the west (Psalm 103:12) and washes us clean (Isaiah 1:18).

Repentance is more than just regret. True repentance is agreeing with God about our sin. It is admitting that our wrongdoing is rebellion against a holy God. More than that, true repentance always leads to a change in action. It involves turning away from sin and turning toward God. The book of Acts describes it this way: "All must repent of their sins and turn to God—and prove they have changed by the good things they do" (Acts 26:20). Are you ready to call your sin what it is and turn away from it?

He is so RICH in *kindness* & *grace* that he purchased our FREEDOM with the blood of his Son and forgave our sins.

EPHESIANS 1:7

Whatever you have done, God will forgive you. In the space above, repent of your sins and receive God's forgiveness. You might want to write down things you're sorry for and then cross them out as a symbol of God erasing your sins.

JUST ASK!

Dear Lord, I really want a new bike, preferably a shiny pink one with streamers on the handles. Did you ever pray like that when you were younger? Maybe you still do, only the prayers have turned into *Please give me a boyfriend.*

Is it okay to pray like that? Well, kind of. Jesus said, "If you remain in me and my words remain in you, you may ask for anything you want" (John 15:7). Did you hear that? We can ask for anything, and that includes bikes and boyfriends. But let's not get so caught up in the second part of that verse (or in the next part, where it says your request will be granted!) without taking a careful look at the first part of the verse.

The verse says, "If you remain in me and my words remain in you ..." That means that you're walking so closely with Jesus that you know His heart and want what He wants because you trust that He knows best. It also means that you're spending so much time in God's Word that you end up praying Scripture without even meaning to. So yes, go ahead and ask God for anything—as long as you are staying close to Him and allowing Him to guide your prayers. Maybe He wants you to ask for a bike or a boyfriend. But if you ask for those things and sense that He's leading you in another direction, follow where He leads.

"But if you remain in me and my words remain in you, you may ask for anything you want, and it will be granted!"

John 15:7

Here's your chance—in the space above, doodle your requests to God. You can ask for anything!

YIELD TO HIM

If prayer is sort of like entering God's throne room and climbing up into His lap for a talk, the last part of our prayer acronym—yield—is like putting our head on His shoulder and resting. It is us coming to God like a little child and letting Him be God.

When you're driving, a yield sign means to slow down and give someone else the right-of-way. In religious terms, we might call it submission. It is the part of the Lord's prayer where we say, "Your will be done." Basically, yielding is saying to God, "You are God, You know everything and have all power, and so I trust You with everything I've just prayed. If I've asked for something that isn't good, I trust You not to answer my prayer. And if I've forgotten to pray for something, I trust You to do what is best. And if You don't give me what I've asked for, I still trust You and believe that You are good."

If you're having trouble yielding to God, it probably means that your view of God is too small or your view of yourself is too big. Whenever we pray, we should approach God with open hands and open hearts because He is God and we are not. That is where our prayers begin and end. We approach God because He is big and we are small, and we leave our requests at His feet because He is big and we are small.

"Our Father in heaven, may your name be kept holy. May your Kingdom come soon. May your will be done on earth, as it is in heaven."

Matthew 6:9-10

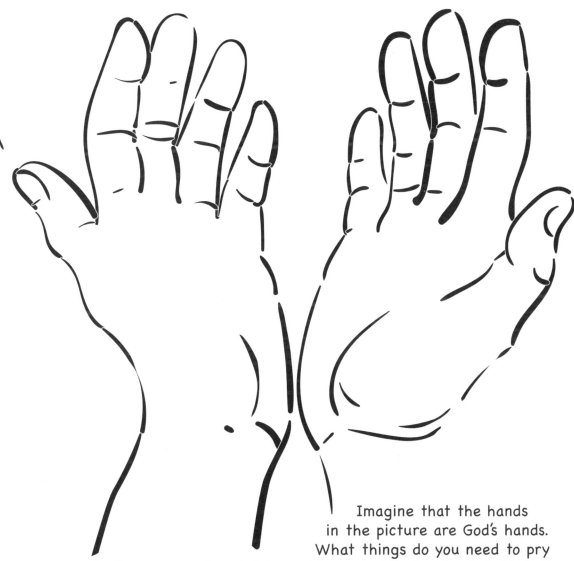

Imagine that the hands in the picture are God's hands. What things do you need to pry out of your own closed fists and leave in the hands of God? Write those things on His hands and trust Him to take care of them in the best possible way—and to keep you in His loving hands no matter what happens.

Worship

WHAT IS WORSHIP?

Imagine for a moment that you are in a terrible car accident, and the first responder on the scene saves your life. Without that person's heroic action, you would have died. How would you respond? My guess is that the moment you regained consciousness in the hospital, you would try to find that person to thank them.

That's what worship is. It is a natural and appropriate response to who God is and what He has done for us. Every person who understands what they have been saved from (eternal separation from God and death) should erupt in praise to God, the one who saved them. Everyone who sees the beauty and masterful perfection of nature should overflow in reverent awe toward the one who made it all. Everyone who studies the Bible and learns about God's perfection, goodness, justice, and mercy should be motivated to praise Him with all of their being and every part of their lives.

Worship can be expressed in many ways: prayer, song, service, giving—anything we do can be offered as a sacrifice of worship to God (1 Corinthians 10:31). Anytime we acknowledge the truth about who God is and adore Him for it, that is worship. In the days ahead we'll talk a little more about specific ways we can worship God.

SINCE WE ARE receiving a KINGDOM that is UNSHAKABLE, let us be & thankful PLEASE GOD by worshiping him with holy fear and awe. HEBREWS 12:28

WORSHIP ON SUNDAYS

There are no lone ranger Christians. The Christian life, as described in the Bible and practiced through the centuries, is not a solitary experience. We were made for relationship and community, and God's people have always gathered together for corporate worship. Church is not a new invention, nor is it optional if we want to be a growing, mature Christian. That's why the Bible describes Christians as interconnected, using metaphors like a body and a building. We need each other.

One of the primary purposes for church is to worship together. Your presence in church actually helps other people worship— and you can learn from them, too. The way you engage with the service can challenge and encourage someone else to have more awe for God or obey Him better. By singing together and listening to the preaching of God's Word, we express our longing for God and learn from one another new ways to express our love for Him.

Next time you go to church, pay attention to the people around you. Look for ways you can help or encourage someone else as you worship. Seek out some wise people who can teach you more about God. Listen to the sermon, take notes, and sing your heart out. Worshiping with other believers is a wonderful gift!

Be filled with the Holy Spirit, singing psalms and hymns and spiritual songs among yourselves, and making music to the Lord in your hearts.

Ephesians 5:18-19

Use the space above for some worship doodles. Maybe you want to write attributes of God, or write a worship song.

Worship on Mondays

When you get your food from the lunch lady at school, what do you usually say in response? If you have good manners, you probably say "thank you" every day. You don't (or at least you shouldn't) only thank her on Mondays and assume that one thank-you will hold you over for the rest of the week.

But isn't that kind of what we do with God? We go to church on Sundays and do the worship thing, and then we kind of forget to praise Him the rest of the week. Maybe we read our Bible and mutter some prayers asking Him for stuff, but we rarely actually worship Him on any day other than Sunday.

That is not how it should be. Every day God makes the sun rise and gets you out of bed. Every day He forgives your sin and provides for your needs. Every day He listens to you and cares about what happens to you. Without Him, you could not even take your next breath. So how about if you increase your worship quotient for the week? Try one of these ideas, or come up with your own: every day this week, sing a song of praise while you're in the shower. Find something to thank God for each night before bed. After you read your Bible, spend a few minutes thinking about how great God is and telling Him so. Worship is all of life, not just Sundays.

Dear brothers and sisters, I plead with you to give your bodies to God because of all he has done for you. Let them be a living and holy sacrifice the kind he will find acceptable. This is truly the way to worship him.

Romans 12:1

Worship
To ~~Do~~ Today:

Your turn: doodle some ways you can worship God with all of your life, not just on Sundays.

STYLE VERSUS SUBSTANCE

If you take a look at many of our churches, the way we worship seems to be more about self-expression or entertainment than about God. We use the latest technologies and music trends to make our "worship time" appealing. Sometimes it verges on manipulation, where the music is designed to arouse our emotions without engaging our minds.

Now, we worship a creative God who loves beauty, and our love for art is part of the image of God implanted within us. Worship, especially in church, should be done with excellence and beauty, as befits such an amazing God.

But that isn't really what worship is. True worship has to do with what is in our hearts, not whether we raise our hands or how beautifully we sing or what style of music we prefer. Jesus said, "God is Spirit, so those who worship him must worship in spirit and in truth" (John 4:24). In other words, it doesn't matter where we worship or what expression our worship takes. What matters is that we are worshiping the true God, as revealed in the Bible, and that our hearts and minds and spirits are engaged. In practical terms, that means that if our hearts are in the right place, we can worship God even if the song we're singing in church doesn't really touch us. As long as we consciously engage our heart and mind in praise to the living God, we are worshiping.

"God is *Spirit*,
so those who *worship* HIM
must worship in spirit and in *truth*."

John 4:24

Think about your last
worship experience in church.
Were you worshiping in
spirit and truth? In the
space above, jot down
some ideas for practical
ways you can prepare
your mind and heart for
worship next Sunday.

TRY SOMETHING NEW

We've talked a lot in this book about how God made each of us different, and that carries over into worship as well. Each of us has a worship personality—a way that we naturally find it easy to worship God. For some of us, a walk in nature makes us break out into song. For others, studying the Bible and learning something new about God is reverent and worshipful. For still others, it is music—and that can range from hymns to Christian rock music.

Have you given much thought to your worship personality? Chances are, you haven't. Most of us just worship at church and don't give much thought to how we prefer to worship, other than maybe complaining that the songs are too old or the organ is too loud.

This week, spend some time considering when you've felt closest to God and overflowed with awe and worship. Was it in church? On vacation? In your room? Looking at a piece of art? Reading a book? Was it with other people, or by yourself? What was it about that experience that helped you worship? Once you've figured out the way you worship best, try out some new ways of worshiping—especially some that don't come naturally to you—and see what you can learn from them.

As they listen, their secret thoughts
will be exposed, and they will fall to their
knees and worship God, declaring,
"God is truly here among you."

1 Corinthians 14:25

The Scripture verse above describes authentic,
meaningful worship. When and where have you experienced that?
Doodle your thoughts about how you worship best, or describe
the time you felt God was truly there with you.

Week

12

No Secret Christians

SALTY AND SWEET

One of the best flavors ever invented (well, at least in my opinion) is salted caramel. I don't think it even existed ten years ago, and now we have salted caramel everything—from ice cream to facial scrubs and candles. I think it's the mixture of salty and sweet that makes it so magical.

Actually, salty and sweet is a good analogy for the way Christians are supposed to act toward those who don't yet know Jesus. First, we should be salty, as Jesus said (Matthew 5:13). That means we should make people thirsty for Jesus and bring a zap of flavor to all of life. People should see in us a zest for living that comes from knowing the true life that is only found in Jesus, and it should make them want to learn more about Him. But we should also be sweet—kind and engaging and gentle. Too much salt can be abrasive and unappetizing, but when you add in some sweetness, it is the perfect blend.

The way we talk to people, the way we react when we're frustrated, and even the kind of entertainment we seek out should all have the perfect blend of salted caramel witness. Make others see how wonderful, joy-filled, and fun life with Jesus can be! Show them the love of Jesus and make them want to learn more about Him.

"You are the salt of the earth. But what good is salt if it has lost its flavor? Can you make it salty again? It will be thrown out and trampled underfoot as worthless."

Matthew 5:13

Are you making people thirsty for Jesus? Are you showing them how sweet life can be with the One who loves them more than they can imagine? Doodle some ways you can be even more sweet and salty to help others want more of Jesus.

A FRAGRANCE OF JOY

Try to describe the scent of your favorite flower to your friend. It's not easy, is it? Scents are something we have to experience for ourselves. And the funny thing is, they are an experience we can't choose. Think about it: you're walking down the street, and suddenly you smell skunk. Even if you plug your nose, you can't un-smell it, can you? The sense of smell is so immediate that it only takes one breath of apple pie to bring you back to visits at your grandma's house. Or one sniff of sunscreen to remind us of summer days spent at the beach.

The apostle Paul used this overwhelmingly powerful sense to illustrate an important truth about Christians: everywhere we go, we leave behind the aroma of Christ. It comes off in the way we interact with people or the way we react to our circumstances. But the same scent is interpreted differently by different people. To those who love God it is the scent of life, but to those who do not love God it is the scent of death because it makes them feel guilty about their sin.

You can't control how you are perceived by others, but you can control whether the scent you leave behind is one of peace and joy that comes from your faith in God, or one of the rottenness that comes from sin. Who you are on the inside comes out through your actions and attitudes, even when you're not thinking about it.

Our lives are a Christ-like fragrance rising up to God.
But this fragrance is perceived differently by those who are being
saved and by those who are perishing. To those who are perishing, we
are a dreadful smell of death and doom. But to those who are
being saved, we are a life-giving perfume.

2 Corinthians 2:15-16

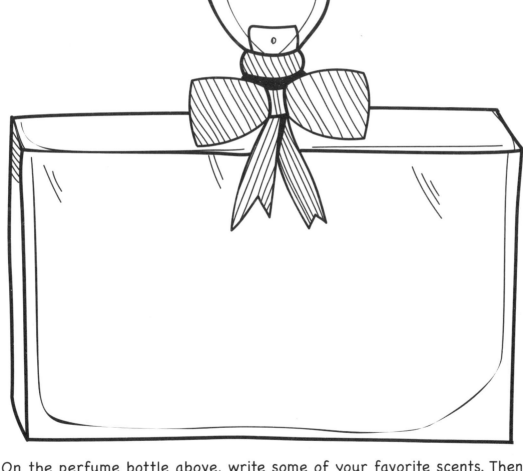

On the perfume bottle above, write some of your favorite scents. Then
think about what kind of scent you are leaving behind as you go about
your day. How can you be the aroma of Christ everywhere you go?

MISSIONARIES AND THE REST OF US

Does your church send out missionaries? If so, what's your impression of them? I grew up thinking they wore outdated clothes and were a little socially awkward—and as a result, I didn't really want to be one of them. First off, let's give them a break. I mean, that prayer card picture is probably 5 years old, so if their clothes look outdated, that's probably why. But more importantly, if you are a Christian, you are a missionary too. So whatever you're thinking about missionaries . . . well, right back atcha.

Missionaries are people just like you. They are not super-spiritual. In fact, the only difference between you and them is that God has sent them somewhere else. You actually have the same job they do—to tell others about Jesus. In the next few days we'll talk about how to do that, but in the meantime, let's get straight what our mission is.

Just before He went back to heaven, Jesus gave the disciples—all disciples, including you and me—a commission. He told them to tell all people everywhere about God's love, Jesus' sacrifice for them on the cross, and the new life they can have in the Holy Spirit. That's it. That's what your life is supposed to be about, whether you live in Akron, Ohio, or Timbuktu.

"Go and make disciples of all the nations, baptizing them in the name of the Father and the Son and the Holy Spirit. Teach these new disciples to obey all the commands I have given you. And be sure of this: I am with you always, even to the end of the age."

Matthew 28:19-20

On the missionary prayer card above, write what your missionary service looks like. Are you a student? Do you help with your youth group or lead a Bible study? Use this doodle as a way to refocus your vision for how you can obey the Great Commission right where God has called you to be right now.

SHARING YOUR STORY, PART 1

Social media and culture in general encourages us to share our story. The idea is that each of us is a star in our own special drama, and that what we do is of immense importance. The truth is that you are important, and loved beyond imagining by the Creator of the universe, but your story is just one tiny part of God's big story. You matter because you are part of His story. What is God's big story? Here it is, in a nutshell:

God is the King, the one who created everything and sustains it by His power. We are His creatures, and He loved us so much that He gave us the choice to love and obey Him or become our own little rulers. Sadly, we chose to rebel against His rule, and as a result we are deserving of eternal death and separation from God.

But God still loves us, and so He moved heaven and earth to save us. He came to our wicked little world, took on flesh, lived a human life in all its misery but did not sin, and then died in our place so that we can be with Him forever. Now, all we have to do is admit that God is the King and we are sinners who deserve death, trust in Jesus' death on the cross to save us, and choose to live for Him. If we accept that free gift of salvation through Jesus, we will be with God forever.

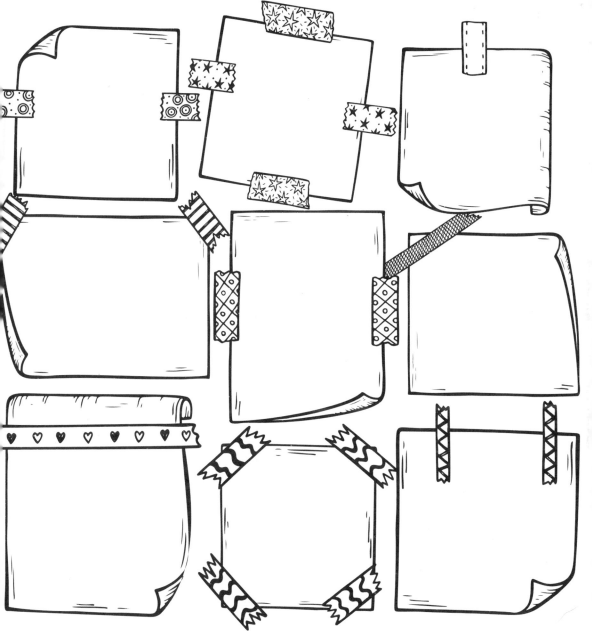

In the notes above, draw a storyboard presentation of the gospel message. You may use fewer or more than the notes provided, but this is a start. The goal is to teach yourself to communicate the good news of salvation in a way that is easy enough for someone with no previous Bible knowledge to understand. Be patient—it may take you a few tries to figure out an approach that works for you.

SHARING YOUR STORY, PART 2

Write your testimony

Yesterday we talked about how to share the gospel—the good news about Jesus—with someone who hasn't heard or understood it before. That's something that every Christian needs to have ready so that we can share it at a moment's notice.

But there is more to the story. People want to hear the story of how Jesus saved *you* and what your life is like now that you know Him. Your personal story is often more touching than a simple gospel presentation. People want to know what difference Jesus makes to *you* before they will be open to hearing what difference He might make for *them*.

On the next page, start brainstorming things you can share from your own story that communicate the gospel in a personal way. Perhaps you have a before-and-after story about the dramatic difference between your life before you were a Christian and what it looks like now. Or perhaps you've experienced deep heartache or a struggle against sin that Jesus has used to demonstrate His love. Whatever your story, God is in it—look for the places you've seen Him work in your heart and tell someone about it.

TODAY'S NEWS

JESUS CHANGED MY LIFE